In honor of

Lisa Shahim

*for supporting the
CALS Foundation
2016*

SCIENCE
FUNDAMENTALS

THE SCIENCE OF
SPACE

AUTHOR:
MASON CREST

MASON CREST

MASON CREST
450 Parkway Drive, Suite D
Broomall, PA 19008
(866) MCP-BOOK (toll free)
www.masoncrest.com

First printing
1 3 5 7 9 8 6 4 2

Library of Congress Cataloging-in-Publication Data

The science of space.
    pages cm. — (Science fundamentals)
Audience: Age 14.
Audience: Grades 7 to 8.
Includes bibliographical references and index.
ISBN 978-1-4222-3515-7 (hc) — ISBN 978-1-4222-8335-6 (ebook)
1. Space and time—Juvenile literature. 2. Space sciences—Juvenile literature.
3. Outer space—Exploration—Juvenile   literature.
QC173.59.S65S43 2017
523—dc23
2015035345

Science Fundamentals Series ISBN: 978-1-4222-3512-6

SCIENCE FUNDAMENTALS

THE SCIENCE OF ENERGY
THE SCIENCE OF LIFE
THE SCIENCE OF SPACE
THE SCIENCE OF TIME

PICTURE CREDITS

Page:
5, 6, 8, 9, 38: Used under license from Shutterstock, Inc.; 10: Bibliothèque Nationale, Paris); 13, 14, 15, 16, 20, 21, 25, 26: Wellcome Library, London; 22, 35: NASA; 27: T.A. Rector (NOAO/AURA/NSF) and Hubble Heritage Team (STScI/AURA/NASA); 30: NASA/JPL-Caltech/ESA/Harvard-Smithsonian CfA, 31: NASA & ES, 32: NASA/JPL-Caltech 33: NASA/ESA/Hubble, 39: NASA / WMAP Science Team, 40: Danor Aharon / Shutterstock.com

Vector Illustrations: 7,12, 19, 23, 29, 37, 43: rzarek/Shutterstock.com

Background Images: 2, 6, 18, 30, 46: TairA/Shutterstock.com; 8, 22, 28, 34, 38: getvitamin/Shutterstock.com; 10, 16, 24, 36, 40: jupeart/Shutterstock.com; 13, 27, 45: Maria Starovoytova/Shutterstock.com; 14, 21, 32, 42, 48: dalmingo/Shutterstock.com

Table of Contents

KEY ICONS TO LOOK FOR:

Words to Understand: These words with their easy-to-understand definitions will increase the reader's understanding of the text, while building vocabulary skills.

Sidebars: This boxed material within the main text allows readers to build knowledge, gain insights, explore possibilities, and broaden their perspectives by weaving together additional information to provide realistic and holistic perspectives.

Research Projects: Readers are pointed toward areas of further inquiry connected to each chapter. Suggestions are provided for projects that encourage deeper research and analysis.

Text-Dependent Questions: These questions send the reader back to the text for more careful attention to the evidence presented there.

Series Glossary of Key Terms: This back-of-the book glossary contains terminology used throughout this series. Words found here increase the reader's ability to read and comprehend higher-level books and articles in this field.

Chapter 1

HIGHWAY TO THE UNKNOWN

Astronomy, the study of all that lies beyond the Earth's atmosphere, may be the most ancient of the sciences. Its roots lie in our desire to order and understand our lives.

Almost certainly you will have looked up at the night sky at some time or another and thought about what you could see there. In doing so you are no different from the very first people, who must also have looked with wonder on the twinkling, unreachable lights far above their heads. The path towards an understanding of what goes on beyond our tiny planet has been a long one and we haven't reached its end yet. In this book we will retrace that path and try to see where it may be leading. Many great people have walked it, all of them pushing our knowledge of the Universe further and further out. Today, we are reaching for the beginning of time and the edge of space.

HEAVENLY CLOCKS

Before people could write down their ideas they knew about the phases of the Moon and the changing positions of the Sun and stars. The constant regular motion of the Sun, Moon and stars were our ancestors' clocks, and because they were so important they were thought to have great powers. For the peoples of many societies these heavenly bodies were gods. Six thousand years ago, for example, people in northern Europe built long graves, called barrows, which were aligned towards the point on the horizon where bright stars were known to rise.

The positions of the stars guided people in their day-to-day lives. Science and religion were linked in the ancient world and an astronomer-priest was a powerful man in his society. By closely observing the sky he could appear to foretell the future. When the star Sirius rose in the east just before dawn, for example, the Ancient Egyptians knew that the River Nile was about to flood.

The peoples of the ancient world divided the stars into groups called constellations, which reminded them of gods and heroes. This is the hunter Orion.

If these things happened when the stars were in the right positions, could it be because it was the stars that *caused* them to happen? It was from such notions that the art of **astrology** came into being. Modern astronomers believe there is no scientific basis for astrology: the planets and the stars have no influence on life on Earth. Yet still a surprising number of people make time to read their horoscopes in the daily newspapers. Some beliefs die hard.

Astrology is not the only discredited belief about the Universe, although some ideas persisted for better reasons. We no longer believe that the Earth is at the center of the Universe, or that it floats on an endless ocean, or that the stars are fixed to the inside of a sphere. Yet perhaps some of the ideas that are now being put forward to explain the Universe are no less extraordinary.

WORDS TO UNDERSTAND

astrology—a belief in the power of the stars and planets to influence people's lives.

astronomy—the study of everything that lies beyond the Earth's atmosphere.

RESEARCH PROJECT

Find out about the Antikythera mechanism, an ancient device invented by an unknown Greek astronomer that could be used to predict the positions of stars and planets. Write a two-page report about the Antikythera mechanism and present it to your class.

TEXT-DEPENDENT QUESTIONS

1. What did ancient humans use to keep time?

2. What is a barrow?

Chapter 2

THE CELESTIAL SPHERES

For thousand of years stargazers and astronomers have made maps and imagined models of the heavens.

The first astronomers whose records we can still find were the Ancient Egyptians and the Chinese. In 1990 a Chinese star map painted on the roof of a tomb was uncovered. The map is over 2,000 years old and may have been painted by the emperor's court astrologer. Although the Chinese were first-class observers they were not scientists. They did not attempt to explain what they saw. The Chinese saw events in the natural world mirroring those in human society; both were intricate and could not be predicted in advance. They believed that nature is far too complicated for us to understand and it is pointless to try. The Chinese Universe was a magical place in which the idea that nature is governed by general laws played no part.

ASTRONOMY AND RELIGION

Although observations of the sky played a big part in their lives, the Egyptian astronomers took us no further towards an understanding of what moved the Universe. They may have produced one of the most advanced calendars in the ancient world, more than 4,500 years ago, but their view of the Universe was based on religion rather than on science. The Ancient Egyptians believed the Sun was the god Ra crossing the sky in his rowing boat, for example.

In the Near East the Babylonians, living in what is now Iraq, drew up a remarkable series of astrological charts over 3,000 years ago. Among

Over hundreds of years, ancient astronomers in Mesopotamia kept track of the movement of stars and planets in order to predict eclipses or calculate the dates of important events. Their observations were recorded on clay tablets such as the one pictured here.

them were detailed lists of the rising and setting times for the planet Venus. Drawing up these lists would have required careful observation over a very long period. Yet the Babylonians were interested in little more than predicting events in the sky so that they could forecast events on Earth. For all its sophistication, Babylonian astronomy had more to do with fortune-telling than science. For the first genuine attempts at a scientific, reasoned explanation for what was happening above their heads, we have to turn to the Ancient Greeks.

WHAT IS THE UNIVERSE MADE OF?

The Greek philosopher Thales lived in the town of Miletus, in what is now Turkey, around 600 BCE. He is generally credited as being the first person we know who tried to answer the question, "What is the Universe made of?" without giving an answer that depended on the supernatural. His solution was, to us, unexpected. The Universe, Thales said, is made of water and the Earth floats in an infinite ocean. He must have been aware of, and influenced by, the beliefs of the Babylonians and Egyptians. Water was vital to the peoples of the ancient world and it should be no surprise that it was given such an important role.

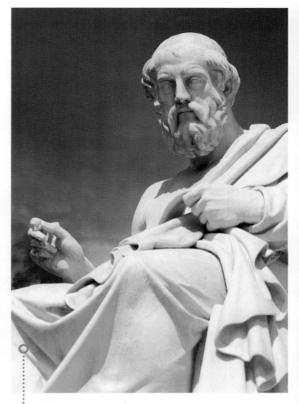

Plato, one of the greatest of the ancient Greek thinkers, believed that the planets moved in perfect circles.

Thales's pupil Anaximander attempted to draw a map of the whole Earth. It had been long been observed that the stars seen from the northern hemisphere appear to rotate around Polaris, the Pole Star. Anaximander imagined the sky as spheres surrounding the Earth, with the stars on an inner sphere and the Sun and Moon on an outer one. He disagreed with Thales about what the Universe was made of, asking where the water was in things that were hot and dry. Instead, he said that all things arose from a **fundamental essence**, which was featureless, and unlike anything else.

Other thinkers tried to describe the Universe in terms of what was familiar to them. At various times it was said to be made of air, or earth, or fire, as well as of water. Empedocles, who lived in Acragas on the island of Sicily, around

450 BCE, put these ideas together and said that all things were a mixture of air, earth, fire and water. Empedocles is credited as being the first to suggest, after examining a **meteor**, that the Earth and stars are made from the same materials.

THE MUSIC OF THE SPHERES

One of the greatest Greek thinkers was Plato. His ideas influenced thought long after his death. Plato was born in Athens around 427 BCE. He declared that the heavens were perfect and so the stars and planets must move in "perfect curves on perfect solids," circles around spheres, in other words. He believed that the spheres made music as they turned, an idea that persisted for many centuries.

However, Plato's **celestial spheres** did not fit what most people actually observed. Sometimes the planets did funny things; they looped backwards in their paths before turning back and carrying on in the first direction again. How was this to be explained? The Greeks were reluctant to give up what seemed a good idea. The astronomer Eudoxus came up with a complex scheme that involved spheres moving within spheres within yet more spheres, all rotating in slightly different directions.

Around 260 BCE the astronomer Aristarchus came up with an idea that was way ahead of its time. The Earth wasn't the center of the Universe at all, he said, everything went around the Sun. This explained the observations that had been made of the planets, without having to resort to Eudoxus's complex theories. Since the stars appeared not to move, apart from motion that was due to the Earth rotating beneath them, Aristarchus reasoned that this must be because they are infinitely far away. These notions seemed much too far-fetched for the people of the time and his ideas were rejected.

Belief in celestial spheres, with the Earth at the center, persisted. Other schemes were put forward, such as having the planets orbit the Sun, which in turn orbited the Earth, carrying the planets with it. Around 100 CE a book was published that summarized astronomical thinking up until then. This was the *Almagest*, written by the astronomer Ptolemy.

Ptolemy's universe looked like this: the Earth was at the center and around it, in increasing order of distance, were the Moon, Mercury, Venus, the Sun, Mars, Jupiter and Saturn. The planets were attached to little spheres, and moved in circles called **epicycles**. The little spheres were attached to larger spheres surrounding the Earth. The stars were fixed to an eighth sphere surrounding the others. It has to be said that this system worked! It could be used to predict accurately where the planets would be in the sky and, more importantly, it gave reasons why.

Astronomy seemed to be more or less stuck after this. It would be another 1,400 years before more accurate observations made it necessary to find a better explanation.

In his book *Almagest*, the Egyptian mathematician and astronomer Claudius Ptolemy proposed ideas about the structure of the Universe that would persist for more than 1,400 years. This sixteenth-century Portuguese map based on Ptolemy's concept of "celestial spheres" shows the Earth at the center, with spheres for the Moon (Luna, believed at that time to be a planet), Mercury, Venus, the Sun, Mars, Jupiter, and Saturn. The ring labeled "Firmamento" was thought to contain all the stars.

WORDS TO UNDERSTAND

celestial spheres—crystal spheres upon which the planets and stars were thought to move by the Ancient Greeks. There are no spheres, but astronomers today sometimes use the idea of a celestial sphere to describe the positions of objects in space in relation to the Earth.

epicycle—a small circle, the center of which rolls around a larger circle.

fundamental essence—an idea put forward by the Greek philosopher Anaximander. This was the mysterious substance from which all other materials in the Universe came.

meteor—a streak of light in the night sky caused by a rocky particle from space glowing white hot through friction as it enters the Earth's atmosphere. A meteor big enough to pass through the atmosphere and strike the surface is called a meteorite.

RESEARCH PROJECT

Using the Internet or your school library as a guide, create a model of the "celestial spheres" proposed by Ptolemy. Include the ecliptic path, or route that the Sun follows through the sky from Earth's perspective.

TEXT-DEPENDENT QUESTIONS

1. What did the ancient Egyptians believe about the Sun?

2. What was Ptolemy's concept of the Universe?

Chapter 3

REVOLUTIONS

In the sixteenth and seventeenth centuries people began to question the accepted ideas about the Universe.

○ The sixteenth-century Polish astronomer Copernicus suggested that the Earth went around the Sun—an idea considered sacrilegeous to religious authorities of his time.

In 1543 astronomy was kicked out of its long slumber when a book called *On the Revolutions of the Celestial Spheres* was published. Its author, the astronomer Nicholas Copernicus, was born in Torun, Poland, in 1473. In 1507 it occurred to Copernicus that it would be much easier to work out the positions of the planets if he assumed that the Sun was at the center of the Universe and that the planets, including the Earth, went around it. As we have seen, this was not entirely a new idea. Aristarchus had suggested it almost 1,800 years earlier. Copernicus began to work out the details of his new system and found that it explained some of the puzzling aspects of planetary movement, such as why some planets occasionally seemed to travel backwards.

If the Earth was going around the Sun in a smaller orbit than Mars, Jupiter and Saturn, then every so often it would overtake them. They would appear, from our point of view, to be going in reverse.

The Copernican system was much simpler than Ptolemy's and yet Copernicus still believed that the planets must move in perfect circles on solid celestial spheres. This meant that his system had to have some epicycles built in, too. In effect, Copernicus was really adapting the Greek system rather than overthrowing it. Yet this was an important step away from the view of the Universe that had held sway for so long.

THE SUN-CENTERED UNIVERSE

Copernicus believed that his Sun-centered Universe wasn't just a device for simplifying calculations. He thought the Universe really was like that. Pause for a moment and try to put yourself in the position of someone hearing this idea for the first time. For thousands of years humanity had believed itself to be at the center of creation, and suddenly along had come someone who dared to suggest it wasn't so. Unsurprisingly, it was not a popular suggestion, especially with the Church.

No one at that time willingly made an enemy of the Church, and Copernicus was careful to restrict the circulation of his ideas. He eventually agreed to publish his *Revolutions*, dedicating it to Pope Paul III. When the book was being printed, a minister named Andreas Osiander added an introduction without Copernicus's approval. In it he said that these new ideas need not be considered as true! Copernicus had no opportunity to demand a correction; it is said that he received a bound copy of the book when he was on his deathbed. It was several decades before people discovered that Copernicus hadn't written the introduction.

THE NEW STAR

For some time nothing changed. Many astronomers carried on working with the old, familiar system. Yet word of the new Copernican model began to spread. The idea that the sun goes around the Earth and that the planets go around the Sun was revived by the Danish astronomer Tycho Brahe (1546–1601). Tycho was one of the greatest astronomers of the days before the invention of the telescope. His reputation was made when he published, in 1573, a short book entitled *De Nova Stella*, which means "On the new star." In it Tycho described his observations of a new star that had

A drawing from Copernicus's 1543 book, which shows the Sun at the center of the Universe as planets, including the Earth, revolve around it. Like Ptolemy, Copernicus placed a sphere of stars beyond the sphere of Saturn.

appeared the previous year. We now know that this was not a new star at all, but a star that had suddenly exploded and increased enormously in brightness. Ever since, exploding stars have been called **novas**.

In 1577 Tycho made some detailed observations of a **comet** that appeared in that year. The Ancient Greeks had believed that comets moved through the Earth's atmosphere, but Tycho showed that the comet he had seen must be further away than the Moon. It also seemed that the comet did not move on a circular path, but followed a route that took it *through* the celestial spheres. As a firm believer in the old system, Tycho was not very comfortable with this. In an attempt to explain the comet's behavior, he suggested that all planets, except for the Earth, moved around the Sun.

Towards the end of his life, Tycho heard of the work of Johannes Kepler (1571–1630), one of the first firm supporters of the Copernican view. Tycho was so impressed by the quality of Kepler's work that he invited him to be his assistant. Kepler accepted the position, a decision that was of great importance to the development of astronomy.

Tycho Brahe was probably the greatest astronomer of the age before the telescope. From observatories in the kingdom of Denmark, and later in the city of Prague, Brahe made many detailed observations of the night sky.

THROUGH THE TELESCOPE

In Italy the great scientist Galileo Galilei (1564–1642) had come to believe in Copernicus's ideas and, in fact, exchanged letters with Kepler on the subject. Galileo's great contribution to astronomy began in 1609 when he got hold of a copy of an invention from Holland, the telescope. By modern standards Galileo's telescopes were modest instruments, magnifying a mere 20 to 30 times. Even so, when he pointed his telescope upwards, what he saw must have astounded him.

Galileo discovered that the Moon had mountains and that there were spots on the Sun. The heavens were not as perfect as the Church had taught. Through his telescope the planets appeared to be little discs, but the stars remained points of light. Galileo concluded from this that the stars must be much further away than the planets. He also discovered that there were many more stars than could be seen with the unaided eye. Most sensationally of all, on the night of January 7, 1610, he discovered the moons of Jupiter—proof that not all bodies in space circle the Earth. Jupiter and its moons were like the Solar System in miniature. He also saw, for the first time, that the planet Venus had phases, just like the Moon. This proved that Venus shone by reflecting the light of the Sun. Galileo published his findings in a book called *Starry Messenger*. Kepler received a copy and wrote in support of Galileo's findings. Galileo took his telescope to Rome to demonstrate his discoveries to high-ranking members of the Church and succeeded in winning many of them over, but not enough of them. In February 1616 he was ordered to give up any ideas that the Earth moved. A week later, Copernicus's *On the Revolutions of the Celestial Spheres* was placed on the Catholic Church's list of forbidden books. It stayed there until 1835.

TYCHO'S RECORDS

In Prague Kepler, without the benefit of a telescope, had come to some far-reaching conclusions of his own. As Tycho Brahe's successor, he had gained access to the great astronomer's huge collection of accurate observations following Tycho's death in 1601. Kepler set out on a careful study of Tycho's records, concentrating on those for the planet Mars. He realized that it just wasn't possible to fit the observations of the planet's movements to the idea that it moved in a perfect circle. Mars was moving in a flattened circle, called an **ellipse**.

A circle has only one center and every point on the circle is at the same distance from the center; the diameter of the circle is the same length wherever you measure it. The diameter of an ellipse, on the other hand, varies according to where it is measured. The longest diameter is called the major

Johannes Kepler, an astronomer who studied with Tycho Brahe, used his observations to produce a set of laws, or rules, to explain the movements of the planets.

axis and the shortest is the minor axis. On the major axis are two points called foci (singular: **focus**), which lie at an equal distance from the center of the ellipse. Kepler discovered that the orbit of Mars fitted an ellipse as exactly as he could work out. At one of the foci of his ellipse was the Sun.

KEPLER'S LAWS

When he looked at the orbits of the other planets, Kepler found that they also moved in ellipses, with the Sun at one focus. This led him to his first law of planetary motion: the planets move in ellipses with the Sun at one focus. In 1609, the year Galileo got his first telescope, Kepler published his work in a book called *New Astronomy*. It also included his second law, dealing with the **velocity** of the planets as they travel around the Sun. This law states that an imaginary line joining the Sun and a planet moves over equal areas in equal times, as the planet moves in its orbit. The closer a planet is to the Sun, the faster it moves.

Kepler had finally put an end to the perfect circles of the heavens. Galileo sent Kepler a telescope and he saw for himself the moons of Jupiter. Kepler gave them the name **satellites**, after a word describing people who surround a more powerful person. The name stuck and we still use it today to describe a small body in orbit around a larger one. Kepler tried out his laws on Jupiter's moons and found that they, too, were moving in ellipses. In 1619 Kepler published a third law, relating the distance of a planet from the Sun to the time it takes to complete its orbit.

Kepler tried to work out what the force might be that was controlling the movements of the planets. Not surprisingly, he thought the Sun might have something to do with it, but how was the force transmitted? Kepler thought it might be a form of magnetism: William Gilbert (1540–1603), the physician to Queen Elizabeth I, had recently demonstrated that the Earth acted like a giant bar magnet, but he was unable to produce a satisfactory explanation. That would come some 50 years later from Isaac Newton and his famous work on **gravity**.

Kepler's great work did not get the approval it deserved. In 1632 Galileo published his *Dialogue Concerning the Two Chief World Systems*, setting out in the form of an imaginary conversation the differences between the views of

Ptolemy and Copernicus. There was no doubt that Galileo's sympathies were with Copernicus, yet nowhere did he mention Kepler's findings, which backed up this view. The Church disapproved strongly of Galileo's views and, under threat of torture, he was forced to withdraw his support for Copernicus.

There was no turning back, however. The belief in an Earth-centered Universe would have to be abandoned, despite the efforts of the Church. The scientific revolution that Copernicus had started was not so easily stopped.

 # WORDS TO UNDERSTAND

axis—the line around which an object spins. The Earth's axis runs through it from one pole to the other. An axis is also a line about which an object is symmetrical. An ellipse has a long (major) and a short (minor) axis.

comet—a relatively small object traveling around the Sun in a long, stretched-out orbit. Comets are thought to be "dirty snowballs" about 6 miles (10 km) across. When a comet gets near the Sun a tail forms from gas and dust as part of the comet boils off into space. The tail may be 600,000 miles (1 million km) long.

ellipse—a geometric figure like a flattened circle.

focus—one of two points on the long axis of an ellipse. The sum of the distances from any point on the ellipse to each focus is always the same.

gravity—the phenomenon associated with the gravitational force acting on an object. The weight of an object is determined by the force of gravity acting on it.

nova—a star that becomes over a thousand times brighter in a period of a few days. Novas are believed to be caused in double-star systems when material is transferred from one star to another, resulting in a titanic thermonuclear explosion.

satellite—a small body in space that orbits a larger one. The Moon is a satellite of the Earth and the Earth is a satellite of the Sun.

velocity—velocity usually means the same thing as speed, but in scientific terms a velocity is given by the speed of an object and the direction in which it is traveling.

TEXT-DEPENDENT QUESTIONS

1. Why was Copernicus's idea that the Sun was at the center of the Universe controversial in the sixteenth and seventeenth centuries?

2. What 1610 discovery by Galileo proved that not all bodies in space circled the Earth?

3. What is Kepler's first law of planetary motion

RESEARCH PROJECT

No one is certain who invented the first telescope, but there are several possible candidates. Read about the history of the telescope, and prepare a presentation for your class. Use evidence that you find in library books or on the Internet to support your conclusion about who may have created the first telescope.

Chapter 4

THE UNIVERSAL FORCE

The scientific laws that govern the movements of bodies in space have their origin in the work of a great seventeenth-century scientist, Isaac Newton.

Sir Isaac Newton formulated laws that explained why all objects, from a falling apple to the planets traveling around the Sun, move as they do.

Isaac Newton was born in Woolsthorpe, Lincolnshire, on Christmas Day 1642, the year Galileo died. The story has often been told of Newton sitting in his mother's garden on a moonlit night. He was disturbed by the sound of an apple falling from a nearby tree. The thought came to him, "Why doesn't the Moon fall to Earth, like the apple?" It took genius to come up with the answer—the Moon *is* falling. The force that holds the Moon in orbit around the Earth is the same force that attracts the apple to the ground. Newton reasoned that, in fact, the Moon is falling *around* the Earth. It wasn't enough simply to have such an insight, however, it had to be proved by calculation.

THE DIMINISHING FORCE

Newton was aware of Kepler's laws, which had by then been accepted by scientists. He knew that any explanation he came up with for the motion of both the Moon and the apple would have to explain Kepler's ideas, too. Newton proposed that the rate at which an object falls depends on the strength of the **gravitational force** acting on it. He calculated that the strength of the force acting between two objects changes according to what is known as the **inverse-square law**. As the distance between the objects increases, the force decreases by the distance squared, or multiplied by itself. This means that if the distance doubles, the force is a quarter of what it was; if the distance trebles, the force is cut to a ninth.

To compare the rate at which the apple fell with that of the Moon, Newton had to discover how much further away from the center of the Earth the Moon was than the apple. There was not much information available; there was no accurate measurement of the Earth's size, for example, and the results of his calculations did not agree with what he observed. Newton also had to create a whole new branch of mathematics, calculus, to deal with the numbers involved.

It was 1679 before Newton returned to the problem. His great scientific rival, Robert Hooke, had boasted that he could prove mathematically that, since the planets moved in ellipses, the force pulling them towards the Sun would vary according to the inverse-square law. Newton set about doing the calculations himself. In 1684 the astronomer Edmund Halley, to whom we shall return shortly, tiring of Hooke's continual boasting, went to Newton and asked him if he could prove Hooke's idea. Newton replied that he had done so five years earlier but had mislaid the papers! At Halley's urging Newton did the work again. He showed that if an object in space obeys Kepler's second law then it is being acted upon by a force of attraction, and that if this force obeys the inverse-square law, the path the object follows will be an ellipse.

GRAVITY AND MOTION

Halley persuaded Newton to produce a book setting out his new ideas concerning motion and gravity. After 18 months of hard work Newton published, in 1687, a book that many believe to be the greatest work of science ever written. This was his *Mathematical Principles of Natural Philosophy*, usually referred to as the *Principia*, from its Latin title. Within it Newton

Edmund Halley used Newton's laws of motion to calculate the path of the comet that was named after him. He correctly predicted that it would be seen again 76 years later.

put forward a vision of the Universe in which all events took place against a background of infinite space and smoothly flowing time.

Building on Galileo's experiments with moving objects and Kepler's work on the movements of the planets, Newton set out his three laws of motion. These say that:

1. A moving body will continue to move in the same direction and at the same speed unless something diverts it;
2. Any change in the speed or direction of a moving object depends on the size of the force acting on the object, divided by the mass of the object;
3. For every action there is an equal and opposite reaction.

Newton's theory of gravity, the force that attracts all objects to each other, says that the size of the force is proportional to the objects' masses multiplied together. It also states that the force decreases as the distance between the objects increases, according to the inverse-square law.

Gravity and the laws of motion apply to all objects, whether they be apples falling to Earth or planets orbiting the Sun. Isaac Newton's laws provided the first real explanation for Kepler's laws of planetary motion. Using Newton's laws, Edmund Halley calculated that a comet that appeared in 1682 had followed the same path as a comet seen in 1531 and 1607. He suggested that it was the same comet returning each time and predicted that it would be seen again in 1758. Sure enough, it did return, and though Halley was not alive to see it, the comet was named after him—Halley's Comet. In time, astronomers would show that Newton's laws could be applied to the whole Universe.

Photo of Halley's Comet, taken on its most recent visit to the Earth's neighborhood, in March 1986. The appearance of Halley's comet has been recorded at least 29 times, going back to 239 BCE. After passing beyond the orbit of Neptune, Halley's comet will eventually return in the year 2061.

WORDS TO UNDERSTAND

calculus—a technique for making calculations involving quantities that are changing continuously. This branch of mathematics was developed separately by Sir Isaac Newton and Gottfried Leibniz (1646–1716).

gravitational force—the force that acts between any two objects in the Universe, attracting them to each other.

inverse-square law—a law in which the size of a force is determined by the square of the force. If you treble the distance the force is reduced to a ninth, and if you halve the distance the force increases four times.

TEXT-DEPENDENT QUESTIONS

1. What scientific law did Newton decide affects the strength of the gravitational force between two objects?

2. What are Newton's three laws of motion?

RESEARCH PROJECT

Using the internet or your school library, find out more about one of the following scientists who made important contributions to our understanding of Space: Nicholas Copernicus, Isaac Newton, Tycho Brahe, Galileo Galilei, Johannes Kepler, or Edmund Halley. Write a two-page paper that discusses this scientist's accomplishments, and present it to your class.

Chapter 5

AN INFINITE UNIVERSE?

During the eighteenth and nineteenth centuries the major challenge to astronomers was to answer questions about the size of the Universe.

In 1692, while at Cambridge University, Newton received a letter from the Reverend Richard Bentley. The possibility that the Universe was infinite in size had been discussed for over a hundred years and Bentley said that if this were so then every part of the Universe would feel the pull of gravity. Everything in the Universe should collapse together.

Newton tried to explain this by saying that if the stars were distributed evenly through space then the force of gravity between them would be acting equally in all directions. (Although the force of gravity decreases with distance it never disappears.) The Universe would be balanced and there would be no collapse. He quickly realized, however, that this solution just would not do. If there were the slightest movement of any star the balance would be lost and everything in the Universe would crash together, either in one great pile of stars and planets or in many smaller ones.

OLBERS'S PARADOX

Both Newton and Bentley had made one great error. They had assumed that the stars were stationary. It was Edmund Halley who pointed out, in 1718, that at least three stars—Sirius, Arcturus and Procyon—had shifted from the positions recorded for them on Greek star maps. He concluded that the stars were moving, but because they were so far away the movement only became apparent over many years. The fact that the stars were moving led to the conclusion that they were scattered throughout space and not equal distances apart. It was the motion of the stars that prevented gravity from pulling them all together.

Halley pointed out another problem presented by the idea of an infinite Universe. In 1610 Kepler had written, "in an infinite Universe the stars would fill the heavens." So wherever you looked there would be a star. The entire sky should be shining as brightly as the Sun! The fact that it wasn't led Kepler to believe that the Universe is not infinitely big. The problem became known as Olbers's **Paradox**, after the German astronomer Heinrich Olbers (1758–1840). Olbers suggested that there must be clouds of dust between the stars that hid some of them from our view. But this solution doesn't work. Eventually, the energy from the stars behind the dustclouds would heat them until they glowed and the sky would still be filled with light. The reason the night sky is dark wouldn't be found for another hundred years.

Meanwhile, the end of belief in the sphere of fixed stars led astronomers to investigate how the stars were distributed in space. In 1750 the English astronomer Thomas Wright (1711–1786) tried to explain the appearance of the Milky Way—a band of light in the night sky.

German astronomer Heinrich Olbers asked the question that became known as Olbers's Paradox: "Why is the sky dark at night?" Olbers thought that dustclouds in space might be concealing stars from our sight.

Unfortunately, because of street lights, the Milky Way isn't clearly visible today from our towns and cities; the sky is never dark enough to see it properly. Before the invention of the telescope people thought it was a kind of cloud, but now it had been revealed as a collection of many stars. Wright thought there must be many more stars in the direction of the Milky Way than elsewhere.

MAPPING THE MILKY WAY

In the 1780s William Herschel (1738–1822), one of the greatest astronomers of has age, also turned his attention to the Milky Way and the cloud-like **nebulas**, fuzzy patches of light in the night sky. Ptolemy had recorded six or seven in his catalogue, but with the advent of the telescope more had been discovered. Herschel set out on a 20-year project of star counting and nebula-spotting. He was greatly helped in this work by his sister Caroline (1750–1848), who not only helped William build his telescopes, but was also a skilled astronomer in her own right, discovering eight new comets.

Herschel established his claim to greatness on March 13 1781. On that night he saw, through his telescope, an object that he knew was not a star. To begin with he thought it was a comet. Other astronomers had trouble confirming the existence of this new object, but Herschel's telescopes were the best available at the time. Eventually, the orbit of the object was calculated. This was no comet that Herschel had discovered but a new planet. He was the first person to find a previously unknown planet in recorded history. After much discussion the new planet was named Uranus, though for years it was called "Herschelium" in France, in the astronomer's honour.

In order to draw up a three-dimensional map of the Universe, Herschel assumed first, that his telescope was good enough to see to the furthest reaches of the Milky Way, and second, that the stars were distributed regularly within it. There was no way to calculate the distances to the stars at the time and so astronomers were forced to make guesses. After counting stars in well over 3,000 places in the sky, Herschel produced his first chart, in 1785. The Universe, he believed, was a great disc of stars with the Sun positioned somewhere near the center. The Milky Way was what we could see when we looked out towards the edge of the disc.

The Sun could only be placed near the center of the Universe, but not exactly there. For Herschel had discovered that the Sun, like the other stars, was moving. Almost three centuries before, Copernicus had shown that the Earth could not be at the center of the Universe, and now Herschel had said that the Sun could not be there either.

For some time after Herschel had drawn up his map of the Milky Way, or the **Galaxy** as it was often called (from the Greek word for milk), astronomers got no further in

Caroline Herschel.

Sir William Herschel and his sister Caroline were skilled astronomers. William Herschel gained fame by discovering a previously unknown planet, Uranus, while Caroline discovered several comets during the nineteenth century. This dawing shows them polishing a telescope lens.

The Horsehead Nebula is a huge cloud of gas and dust in space, located in the constellation of Orion about 1,600 light-years from Earth. The radiation from nearby stars makes the gas glow.

determining the structure of the Universe. It was not until 1838 that the first successful measurement of the distance from the Earth to a star was made. In that year Friedrich Bessel (1784–1846), a German astronomer, calculated the distance to the faint star 61 Cygni. He did so by determining its **parallax**.

PARALLAX

Parallax is a measure of how an object appears to shift in position against a more distant background, when viewed from different angles. Try it for yourself. Hold up a finger and, with one eye closed, line up your finger with a tree outside or a book on a shelf. Now look at the finger through the other eye. It will appear in a different position against the background. The amount it seems to move depends on the distance between the finger and your eye. The closer your finger, the further it will move. This effect is called parallax. To calculate the distance to a star Bessel had to make careful measurements of its change in position relative to two fainter and, he assumed, more distant stars, as seen from opposite ends of the Earth's orbit. His answer was a surprise: 61 Cygni was more than 60 million miles (97 trillion km) away, much further than anyone had guessed. Such large numbers are difficult to handle and astronomers soon began to use another unit of measurement—the **light year**. This is the distance light travels in one year—5.88 trillion miles (9.46 trillion km)—making the distance to 61 Cygni roughly 10.3 light years. (Bessel's measurement was not quite right; today scientists believe 61 Cygni is 11.4 light years from Earth.)

Measuring the distances to stars was difficult and required very accurate instruments. By 1900 fewer than 300 distances were known, still far too few to build up a three-dimensional picture of the entire Universe. By this time, however, astronomers had a new tool at their disposal—the camera. Photographic film could be made that was more sensitive than the human eye and images of very faint objects could be captured. From 1878 onwards Jacobus Kapteyn (1851–1922) spent 12 years measuring the positions of stars recorded on photographic plates taken by the Scottish astronomer David Gill (1843–1914). Kapteyn published a catalogue of more than 450,000 stars in the sky over the southern hemisphere. From his star counting Kapteyn concluded that the Galaxy was shaped like a disc, just as Herschel had thought. He believed it to be 55,000 light years in diameter and 11,000 light years thick.

STAR STREAMS

Kapteyn went on to study the motion of the stars. Until then, astronomers thought that the stars moved around randomly, but Kapteyn discovered that the stars divided into two streams: three-fifths of them were moving in one direction and the remainder were moving in the opposite direction. Kapteyn could not explain these results and it was a student of his, Jan Oort (1900–1992), who eventually provided the answer—the Galaxy is spinning around its center.

Oort said that, because the Galaxy is not a solid disc, all the stars in it do not rotate at the same speed. Those nearer the center move faster than those towards the outside. The stars closer to the center of the Galaxy than the Sun are going faster and overtake us, while those further out fall behind us as we overtake them. Kapteyn's two star streams represent the central stars moving ahead and the outermost stars falling behind. The Sun, for example, takes 200 million years to complete one circuit of the Galaxy.

 ## RESEARCH PROJECT

To understand parallax, hold a pencil at arm's length. As you alternately open and close each eye, the pencil appears to move relative to the background. The closer you hold the pencil, the larger the movement of the pencil appears to be. If you know the distance between each eye and the angle of the apparent movement (the parallax angle), you can calculate how far away the pencil is.

WORDS TO UNDERSTAND

galaxy—a huge assembly of tens of billions of stars, gas and dust held together by gravity.

light year—the distance light travels through free space in one year. It is equivalent to 5.88 trillion miles (9.46 trillion km).

nebula—originally used to describe any fuzzy area of light visible through a telescope, this term is now used for huge clouds of gas and dust between the stars.

paradox—a paradox is a situation that doesn't make sense or goes against what we believe to be true or possible.

parallax—the apparent movement of a distant object against a more distant background when viewed from two different positions.

TEXT-DEPENDENT QUESTIONS

1. Why did Edmund Halley believe that the Universe was not infinitely large?

2. What planet did William Herschel discover in 1781?

3. What is the name for the galaxy in which Earth is located?

Chapter 6

FURTHER OUT AND FURTHER BACK

At last, by the beginning of the twentieth century, astronomers had a reliable way of measuring the vast stellar distances.

In the 1910s Henrietta Leavitt (1868–1921), one of a group of pioneering American women astronomers, discovered that the brightness of a group of stars called **Cepheid variables** was related to the time each star took to go through a complete cycle from bright to dim and back to bright again. (A variable star is one that changes in brightness over a regular period.) The brighter the star, the longer it took to go through its cycle. A simple calculation, based on how bright the star appeared to be, allowed Leavitt to work out the star's distance from the Earth.

Then, in 1914, Harlow Shapley (1885–1972), another American, began a study of collections of stars called **globular clusters**. These consist of between ten thousand and a million stars, including some Cepheid variables, in a roughly spherical arrangement. By using Leavitt's method he discovered that a typical globular cluster was some 50,000 light years away; in 1916 he found one that was almost 100,000 light years distant. To take account of measurements such as these, the Universe would have to be ten times bigger than the size Kapteyn had calculated. Shapley also discovered that the globular clusters were not evenly spread across the sky and he decided that the center of the Galaxy must lie where these clusters were most dense. Harlow's careful observations led him to the conclusion that the Sun wasn't at the center of the Milky Way but was some way out towards the edge. The Earth seemed to be taking up a place in the Universe that was less and less important. Scientists had suspected

A spiral galaxy known as Messier 81, located about 12 million light-years away from Earth. It is one of the brightest galaxies that can be seen from Earth through telescopes.

for some time that at least some nebulas were made up of collections of very distant stars. The question was whether or not they were part of the Milky Way. In 1913 photographic evidence pointed towards the Milky Way being spiral-shaped, and so were many of the nebulas, but people thought these were just smaller patterns within the larger pattern of the Milky Way.

BEYOND THE MILKY WAY

Most people, including Shapley, thought that everything in the Universe was contained within the Milky Way and that there was nothing else beyond it. Others were considering a different possibility. In 1914, the American astronomer Heber Curtis had described the spiral nebulas as being "inconceivably distant galaxies or universe of stars." The breakthrough came when astronomers found evidence of novas on the photographs they took

of nebulas. The novas were far less bright than would have been expected had they been inside the Milky Way. Curtis estimated that they must be a hundred times more distant, and therefore far outside the Galaxy.

So who was right? Shapley said the spiral nebulas were fairly small and inside the Milky Way galaxy. Curtis said they were big enough to be considered as galaxies in their own right and lay far beyond the Galaxy. In 1920 the two men met to hold a debate on the size of the Universe, but they came to no clear conclusion. The matter was settled in 1923 when Edwin Hubble (1889–1953), an American astronomer, using the most

Galaxies are classified by their shapes. Elliptical galaxies can be nearly circular, while others are thin ellipses. Spiral galaxies can have two arms or many, like our own Milky Way, or there may be a line of stars, called a bar, running through the central nucleus of the galaxy.

powerful telescope in the world at that time, managed to make out stars in the Andromeda galaxy. Hubble went on to show that some of the stars were variables and that their distance could be calculated using Leavitt's findings. He estimated the distance to the Andromeda galaxy to be 800,000 light years, far beyond the Milky Way. Science had to wait 20 years before it was

The Andromeda galaxy is approximately 2.5 million light years away, making it one of the closest galaxies to our Milky Way. This enormous spiral galaxy is 260,000 light-years in diameter.

discovered that Hubble had underestimated the distance to Andromeda, which is, in fact, 2.5 million light years away. Hubble found that other nebulas are even further away, some over a billion light years distant. The Universe is vast beyond anyone's power to comprehend and contains countless billions of galaxies. In 1929 Hubble looked at the velocities of different galaxies and discovered that the speed at which a galaxy is moving away from us depends on how distant it is. The further away it is from us, the faster a galaxy is moving. Hubble thought that the best explanation for this was that the Universe is expanding.

CURVING SPACE

A few years earlier, Albert Einstein (1879–1955) had published his relativity theories—the Special Theory in 1905 and the General Theory in 1915. These theories radically changed the way we look at the Universe. According to Einstein, for example, gravity was not a force acting between bodies, but a distortion in space, caused by the bodies in it. He said that objects pull the space around them out of shape; the bigger the object the more space curves around it. A smaller object, such as a spacecraft, approaching a larger object, such as a planet, would appear to fall towards it. This wouldn't happen because it was being pulled, but because the path it followed through space was curved towards the planet. Gravity is curved space!

In 1919 the idea of curved space was tested during an **eclipse** of the Sun. Einstein had predicted that light traveling towards us from a star would appear to bend as it passed through the strongly curved space close to the Sun. It would only be possible to make such an observation during an eclipse, because otherwise the light of the Sun would drown out the starlight. When the photographs were developed they showed that Einstein had been right, the stars near the Sun did appear to shift.

Einstein's General Theory also said that the Universe had to be either expanding or contracting. He reasoned that a static Universe could not exist, because the curving of space by all the galaxies would cause everything to collapse together. If the Universe was neither static nor collapsing it had to be expanding. Einstein himself, like many others, could not accept this idea. His worry was that, if the Universe was expanding, it had to be expanding rom somewhere. Long ago, the Universe must have started out from a single point, containing all space and time. At this point, called a **singularity**, all the rules we have for understanding the Universe would break down. It would be impossible to work out what came before. Einstein thought this was a nonsensical idea. To avoid it he introduced a "**cosmological constant**" into his equations, a mysterious force that counterbalanced gravity and prevented the Universe from expanding or contracting.

Hubble's discovery of the relationship between how far away galaxies are and their velocities could not be disputed, however. Einstein admitted that he had been wrong, saying the cosmological constant was the biggest blunder of his life. Now the question was, if the Universe was expanding, what was causing it to expand?

The Hubble Space Telescope took this photograph of the Butterfly Nebula, which surrounds a star in the constellation of Scorpio. The gas and space that makes up a nebula could eventually form stars and planets.

EXPANSION OF THE SUPER-ATOM

The first to suggest a possible answer was Georges-Henri Lemaître (1894–1966), a Belgian priest and astronomer. Between 1927 and 1933 he put forward his idea of the "**primordial atom**." He suggested that, far back in time, all the material in the Universe had been in the form of a single super-atom. According to Lemaître this primordial atom started to divide over and over again, eventually forming all the matter in the Universe. He tried to interest Einstein in the idea. Einstein was unimpressed at first, but later came to believe that the idea was a good one. Many others came to share his opinion, but it would be another 30 years before proof was found.

A COOLING UNIVERSE

Then, after the Second World War, a Russian-born scientist named George Gamow (1904-1968) suggested that, in the beginning, the Universe was made up of a substance he called **ylem**. This was an extremely hot "soup" of atomic particles, at a temperature of billions of degrees. For some reason the ylem began to expand and break up. As it expanded it cooled, as the energy it contained was spread over a larger and larger volume of space. Eventually it had cooled enough for all the matter we now see in the Universe to form. In 1948 Ralph Alpher (1921–2007) and Robert Herman (1914–1997) published a scientific paper in which they predicted the **radiation** from the early beginnings of the Universe should still exist. They calculated that this **cosmic background radiation**, as it was called, would have a temperature of about −450°F (−268°C). It was the last faint glow of the unimaginable explosion that gave birth to the Universe. Unfortunately, in the 1940s, there was no way to detect such low temperatures and so the prediction was more or less forgotten for the next 20 years.

In 1950, soon after Gamow published his theory, the English astronomer Fred Hoyle (1915–2001) gave a radio talk. Hoyle was a fierce opponent of the idea of an expanding Universe, believing it to exist in what he called a **steady state**. He mocked Gamow's ideas, describing them as a "big bang." Hoyle had meant the phrase to be insulting, but it stuck in the public's imagination and from then on the beginning of the Universe was called the **big bang**.

For almost 20 years arguments raged between Hoyle's supporters, who believed that the Universe had always existed and had no beginning in time, and those who were believers in the big-bang theory. The end for the steady-state theory came from the new and expanding field of **radio astronomy**.

THE BIRTH OF RADIO ASTRONOMY

Radio astronomy was discovered by accident when, in the 1930s, Karl Jansky (1905–1950), an American radio engineer, detected **radio waves** coming from the center of the Galaxy. Scientists soon discovered that there were many other radio sources in the sky. These are not broadcasts from intelligent life forms elsewhere in the Universe. Radio waves are, in fact, similar to light waves, but they carry less energy. The Sun, for example, gives off energy in the form of invisible radio waves, as well as light and heat.

In the 1950s the Cambridge radio astronomer Martin Ryle (1918–1984) made a map of the radio sources he had detected above the northern hemisphere. If the steady-state theory was correct they should have been distributed evenly through space. However, they were not. The further Ryle looked into space, the more radio galaxies he found. Both the light and the radio waves from distant galaxies have taken billions of years to reach us, and so we see them as they were in the distant past. Astronomers are not simply looking far away, but far back in time, too. Ryle was detecting galaxies as they were closer in time to the big bang. The fact that there were more of them suggested that the Universe had been denser then, with everything closer together. This was tremendous support for the big-bang theory.

In 1964, Robert Wilson (left) and Arno Penzias became the first to detect the cosmic microwave background that occurred shortly after the Big Bang.

EVIDENCE FOR THE BIG BANG

In 1964 Arno Penzias (born 1933) and Robert Wilson (born 1936) made the discovery that finally tipped the scales toward the occurrence of a big bang. They were using a radio antenna to measure **interference** that might obstruct signals arriving from the satellite Echo 1, which had been launched in 1959. They picked up **microwave radiation**, coming from all areas of the sky, which had a temperature equivalent to about −454°F (−270°C). Penzias and Wilson had no idea what it was they had observed and so they contacted the **astrophysicist** Robert Dicke (1916–1997) to ask his opinion. Dicke knew what the pair had found. He had been planning an experiment to detect the background radiation predicted by Alpher and Herman, and he realized that Penzias and Wilson had unknowingly beaten him to it. Penzias and Wilson had detected the remains of the big bang.

The expanding Universe provided the answer to Olbers's paradox. When we look up into the blackest regions of the sky we are looking back to a time when the stars had not yet formed.

RESEARCH PROJECT

Watch the short movie "From the Big Bang to the LHC" (available at "http://education.web.cern.ch/education/Chapter2/Teaching/from-the-big-bang-to-lhc/Globe-movie-I.mp4"http://education.web.cern.ch/education/Chapter2/Teaching/from-the-big-bang-to-lhc/Globe-movie-I.mp4") to find out more about the Big Bang and the origins of space and time.

astrophysicist—someone who studies astrophysics, the study of the physical and chemical changes that take place in planets, stars and galaxies, and other astronomical objects.

big bang—the name given to the theory that all of the matter and energy in the Universe originated in a sudden explosion outwards from a single point around 15 billion years ago.

cepheid variable—a type of star that changes in brightness over a regular period of between 1 and 50 days. The first one was discovered in 1784 in the constellation Cepheus. At the beginning of the twentieth century a method was found to use the brightness of Cepheids in order to measure distances in space.

cosmic background radiation—the faint radiation left over from the big bang explosion. This radiation comes from all points of the sky.

cosmological constant—a factor introduced into his equations by Albert Einstein to balance the force of gravity and ensure that the Universe would neither expand nor contract.

eclipse—an eclipse occurs when light from one object passes through the shadow of another object and is temporarily blocked from view. An eclipse of the Sun occurs when the shadow of the Moon falls on part of the Earth and hides the Sun.

globular cluster—a spherical collection of between 10,000 and a million stars.

interference—interference occurs when two or more waves pass through each other. Where the waves cross they add their energy together. If the crest of one wave coincides with the trough of another they cancel each other out. If two crests coincide they add to give a wave crest that is twice as big. Interference patterns show us where the waves are adding and where they are cancelling. We can see this in the ripples produced when two stones are dropped simultaneously into a pond.

microwave radiation—radiation that is similar to other forms of radiation, such as light waves and radio waves. Microwaves are longer than light waves, but shorter than radio waves. The cosmic background radiation is detected as microwaves.

primordial atom—a cosmic "super-atom" suggested by Georges Lemaître as being the starting point of the Universe. The primordial atom is supposed to have exploded in the big bang. Primordial means "existing at the beginning."

radiation—energy that travels in the form of waves, such as light, microwaves and radio waves. Radiation may also mean a stream of high-energy atomic particles, such as electrons.

radio astronomy—the study of objects in space by detecting the radio waves they give off rather than visible light.

radio waves—a form of low-energy radiation. Radio waves behave in a similar way to light waves, but they are very much longer and special equipment is needed to detect them.

singularity—an infinitely small, infinitely dense point where the laws of physics no longer apply. No one knows what might happen in a singularity: matter, energy, space and time may be destroyed, or created. The entire Universe may have exploded out from a singularity in the big bang.

steady state—the name given to a theory put forward by Fred Hoyle, which states that the Universe has no beginning and no end and maintains much the same appearance. To account for the fact that the Universe is expanding, the steady state theory says that new matter is continually being created from space.

ylem—the name given by George Gamow to the matter that he suggested existed in the early Universe. It was made up of atomic particles in a sea of radiation.

TEXT-DEPENDENT QUESTIONS

1. What astronomer estimated the distance to the Andromeda galaxy to be 800,000 light years?

2. Who proposed the idea of the "primordial atom?"

3. What is radio astronomy?

Chapter 7

BLACK HOLES AND INFLATION

As the search for the edge of the Universe has continued, many scientists have been speculating about the origins of the Universe—and its future.

In 1967 Jocelyn Bell, a graduate student at Cambridge University, noticed something unusual while she was studying records from the Jodrell Bank radio telescope. There seemed to be a rapidly pulsing signal coming from a point in the sky. She made careful observations of the signal and found that the pulses were regularly spaced. Within a few months she had found another one. Some people suggested that these might be signals from far-distant intelligent life and they were jokingly referred to as LGMs ("little green men").

The American astronomer Thomas Gold (born 1920) suggested that the LGMs were **neutron stars**. Astronomers had speculated for some time on the existence of neutron stars. These would come about when a star stopped burning and its immense gravity pulled it in on itself. All the atomic particles in the star would be crushed together forming a superdense mass. In the center of a neutron star a billion tons of material are crushed into a single cubic centimeter.

Giant radio telescopes in the Very Large Array, New Mexico. Radio telescopes collect data on electromagnetic waves emitted from objects in space, such as galaxies and nebulae.

NASA's Wilkinson Microwave Anisotropy Probe (WMAP) was launched in 2001 to map the Cosmic Microwave Background. Data from the spacecraft provided a wealth of data about the origins of the universe 13.7 billion years ago.

As a star collapses it spins faster and faster, like an ice skater spinning around on the ice by bringing in her arms towards her body. As it gets smaller the star's magnetic field becomes more concentrated and more powerful. **Electrons** within the magnetic field are accelerated to nearly the speed of light and give off radiation from the star's north and south magnetic poles. These beams of radiation are like the light beams from a lighthouse, sweeping around. We can only detect the star when one of the beams is pointing directly towards us. This makes the star appear to pulse as the beam passes the Earth, so these stars were soon given the name **pulsars**.

BLACK HOLES

What would happen if a neutron star didn't stop collapsing? In 1928 the Indian astrophysicist Subrahmanyan Chandrasekhar (1910–1955) calculated that if a star was bigger than a certain size, the power of its gravitational force would be greater than the atomic particles in it could resist. It would collapse into a single point, a singularity, bending the space around it so much that nothing, not even light, could escape it. It would become a "**black hole**" in space.

It is impossible to see a black hole directly, but we may be able to see the effect one has on objects near it. Astronomers believe that some very strong sources of radiation, such as the star Cygnus X-1, are the result of material being sucked into a black hole. The Hubble space telescope has detected evidence of a huge black hole three billion times more massive than the sun, at the center of a distant galaxy. Astronomers believe that there are supermassive black holes at the heart of most galaxies, including ours.

In the 1960s the English physicist Stephen Hawking (born 1942) applied the idea of black holes to the whole Universe. In 1970 he wrote a scientific paper with Roger Penrose (born 1931) setting out their belief that the Universe as we see it must have begun as a singularity that marked the beginning of time. If the Universe is like a black hole then everything can be seen as expanding outwards from that first singularity.

Hawking calculated that the Universe ought to be expanding at nearly the same rate in all directions—a notion that seemed to be confirmed by the smoothness of the cosmic background radiation discovered by Penzias and Wilson. In fact, the expansion couldn't have been completely smooth; if it had been there would be no large objects, such as planets, stars and galaxies, in the Universe. There must have been some areas where there was slightly more matter, in order for the galaxies to form. Scientists set about trying to detect variations in the background radiation, which would prove the early Universe had not been smooth.

In 2015, the British physicist Stephen Hawking proposed that black holes may connect to universes that exist parallel to our own.

VOIDS AND RIPPLES

We know that the matter in the Universe is clumped together in different regions. This "lumpiness" in space exists on a massive scale—in 1989 astronomers detected a "Great Wall" of galaxies that covers an area of 500 million to 750 million light years. But they have also found vast volumes of empty space millions of light years across, called **voids**. The structure of the Universe has even been described as resembling soap bubbles, with galaxies on the surface of the bubbles and nothing in the middle.

In 1992 results from the Cosmic Background Explorer (COBE) satellite seemed to show variations in the background radiation for the first time. The results indicated that **"ripples"** had formed in the substance of the Universe within 300,000 years of the big bang. This meant that the Universe had to be denser than scientists had believed, since the greater the amount of material in the Universe, the sooner the ripples would have appeared. Another NASA satellite, the Wilkinson Microwave Anisotropy Probe (WMAP), measured the cosmic background radiation with even greater precision between 2001 and 2010.

The data recorded by these satellites support the **inflationary model** of how the early Universe formed. In this idea, according to the particle physicist Alam Guth (born 1947), a tiny fraction of a second after the Universe appeared it rapidly increased in size, expanding from a region billions of times smaller than an atom to about 10 meters across in less than a trillion trillion trillionth of a second. Such a rapid inflation, Guth said, might have spread "imperfections" through space as matter started to appear in the Universe, which previously had contained only energy. Each of these imperfections might have become a focus around which stars and galaxies formed. One version of the inflationary model pictures our entire Universe as just one among many, an enormous collection of universes stretching on forever.

The COBE and WMAP satellites, along with the Hubble Space Telescope, have also provided evidence for the existence of **dark matter**. This is matter that we cannot detect from Earth. Scientists agree that all the matter that we can observe—planets, stars, and galaxies—make up only about 5 percent of the total material in the Universe. What is the remaining 95 percent of invisible matter? There have been many guesses but, as yet, no firm answers. We are continuing to build up a picture of the Universe that would have astounded Ptolemy, Galileo and Newton—and the picture is not finished yet.

WORDS TO UNDERSTAND

black hole—at the end of its life gravity may cause a massive star to collapse so much that not even light can escape from it. The star becomes invisible, a black hole in space. It may be possible to detect a black hole by the effect it has on objects near it. Many astronomers believe that the star called Cygnus X-1 is orbiting a black hole.

dark matter—matter in the Universe that cannot be detected by our scientific instruments. Some scientists have suggested that there must be more material in the Universe than we can see and that some of it is in the form of invisible dark matter.

electron—a tiny particle, smaller than an atom. Electrons are found in all atoms and also free electrons unattached to anything.

Great Wall—the name given to a vast chain of galaxies extending over 500 million light years, first discovered in 1990.

inflationary model—inflation is a theory of the origin of the Universe that suggests that shortly after the Big bang there was a brief period, lasting a tiny fraction of a second, during which the Universe expanded at a colossal rate. In the course of this inflationary period enormous amounts of energy were produced.

neutron star—a star that has used up all its nuclear fuel and collapsed so much that its atomic particles have been crushed together. If it collapsed any further it would form a black hole.

pulsar—an object far out in space that produces regular pulses of radiation. Pulsars are believed to be rapidly spinning neutron stars.

ripples—faint disturbances in the cosmic background radiation are sometimes referred to as ripples, in the same way as we might refer to ripples on the smooth surface of a pond. Cosmic ripples may show places where the big bang explosion was not quite even. They are unbelievably vast structures. Some are so big that the Universe is not yet old enough for light to have crossed them.

voids—vast volumes of empty space hundreds of light years across.

TEXT-DEPENDENT QUESTIONS

1. What happens to a star as it collapses?

2. Why could the expansion of the Universe not have been completely smooth and uniform?

3. What two NASA satellites measured cosmic background radiation?

RESEARCH PROJECT

Using the Internet or your School library, find out more about the cosmic microwave background radiation. Write a paragraph describing how slight variations in the temperatures in the CMB could lead to the formation of large-scale structures such as stars or planets.

SERIES GLOSSARY OF KEY TERMS

anomaly—something that differs from the expectations generated by an established scientific idea. Anomalous observations may inspire scientists to reconsider, modify, or come up with alternatives to an accepted theory or hypothesis.

evidence—test results and/or observations that may either help support or help refute a scientific idea. In general, raw data are considered evidence only once they have been interpreted in a way that reflects on the accuracy of a scientific idea.

experiment—a scientific test that involves manipulating some factor or factors in a system in order to see how those changes affect the outcome or behavior of the system.

hypothesis—a proposed explanation for a fairly narrow set of phenomena, usually based on prior experience, scientific background knowledge, preliminary observations, and logic.

natural world—all the components of the physical universe, as well as the natural forces at work on those things.

objective—to consider and represent facts without being influenced by biases, opinions, or emotions. Scientists strive to be objective, not subjective, in their reasoning about scientific issues.

observe—to note, record, or attend to a result, occurrence, or phenomenon.

science—knowledge of the natural world, as well as the process through which that knowledge is built through testing ideas with evidence gathered from the natural world.

subjective—referring to something that is influenced by biases, opinions, and/or emotions. Scientists strive to be objective, not subjective, in their reasoning about scientific issues.

test—an observation or experiment that could provide evidence regarding the accuracy of a scientific idea. Testing involves figuring out what one would expect to observe if an idea were correct and comparing that expectation to what one actually observes.

theory—a broad, natural explanation for a wide range of phenomena in science. Theories are concise, coherent, systematic, predictive, and broadly applicable, often integrating and generalizing many hypotheses. Theories accepted by the scientific community are generally strongly supported by many different lines of evidence. However, theories may be modified or overturned as new evidence is discovered.

FURTHER READING

Bauer, Susan Wise. *The Story of Western Science: From the Writings of Aristotle to the Big Bang Theory*. New York: W.W. Norton, 2015.

Bynum, William. *A Little History of Science*. New Haven, Conn.: Yale University Press, 2012.

Dickinson, Terence. *Hubble's Universe: Greatest Discoveries and Latest Images*. Ontario, Canada: Firefly Books, 2012.

Dolnick, Edward. *The Clockwork Universe: Isaac Newton, the Royal Society, and the Birth of the Modern World*. New York: Harper Perennial, 2012.

Heilbron, John L. *Galileo*. New York: Oxford University Press, 2012.

Impey, Chris. *Beyond: Our Future in Space*. New York: W.W. Norton, 2015.

Pohlen, Jerome. *Einstein and Relativity for Kids*. Chicago: Chicago Review Press, 2012.

Schilling, Grovert. *Deep Space: Beyond the Solar System to the End of the Universe and the Beginning of Time*. New York: Black Dog & Leventhal Publishers, 2014.

The Science Book: Everything You Need to Know about the World and How It Works. Washington, D.C.: National Geographic, 2011.

INTERNET RESOURCES

http://www.fnal.gov/pub/science/inquiring/matter

This article on the science of matter, space, and time, with links to additional material, is provided by Fermilab, the premier U.S. particle physics laboratory, which is exploring the smallest building blocks of the matter that makes up the universe.

http://www.nasa.gov

The website of the U.S. space agency has links to news about space exploration, as well as photos and educational videos.

http://www.pbs.org/wgbh/nova/blogs/physics/2015/02/brief-history-speed-light

This web page from the PBS program NOVA provides information about the speed of light.

http://www.biology4kids.com/files/studies_scimethod.html

A simple explanation of the scientific method is available at this website for young people.

http://www.livescience.com

The website Live Science is regularly updated with articles on scientific topics and new developments or discoveries.

https://kids.usa.gov/science/index.shtml

This U.S. government portal includes links to projects and science experiments for young people.

INDEX

Numbers in **bold italics** refer to captions.